DATA ANALYSIS & PROBABILITY – TASK & DRILL SHEETS

Principles & Standards of Math Series

• • • • • • • • • • • • • • • • • • •

Written by Tanya Cook and Chris Forest

GRADES 6 – 8

Classroom Complete Press
P.O. Box 19729
San Diego, CA 92159
Tel: 1-800-663-3609 | Fax: 1-800-663-3608
Email: service@classroomcompletepress.com

www.classroomcompletepress.com

ISBN-13: 978-1-55319-548-1

© 2011

Process Standards Rubric

Data Analysis & Probability – Task & Drill Sheets

Exercise: 1 2 3 4 5 6 7 8 9 10 11 12 13 14 15 — Drill Sheet 1 — Drill Sheet 2 — Review A — Review B — Review C

Expectations
Instructional programs from pre-kindergarten through grade 12 should enable all students to:

GOAL 1: Problem Solving
- build new mathematical knowledge through problem solving;
- solve problems that arise in mathematics and in other contexts;
- apply and adapt a variety of appropriate strategies to solve problems;
- monitor and reflect on the process of mathematical problem solving.

GOAL 2: Reasoning & Proof
- recognize reasoning and proof as fundamental aspects of mathematics;
- make and investigate mathematical conjectures;
- develop and evaluate mathematical arguments and proofs;
- select and use various types of reasoning and methods of proof.

GOAL 3: Communication
- organize and consolidate their mathematical thinking through communication;
- communicate their mathematical thinking coherently and clearly to peers, teachers, and others;
- analyze and evaluate the mathematical thinking and strategies of others;
- use the language of mathematics to express mathematical ideas precisely.

GOAL 4: Connections
- recognize and use connections among mathematical ideas;
- understand how mathematical ideas interconnect and build on one another to produce a coherent whole;
- recognize and apply mathematics in contexts outside of mathematics.

GOAL 5: Representation
- create and use representations to organize, record, and communicate mathematical ideas;
- select, apply, and translate among mathematical representations to solve problems;
- use representations to model and interpret physical, social, and mathematical phenomena.

Process Standards Rubric

Data Analysis & Probability – Task & Drill Sheets

Drills

	Warm-up 1	Timed Drill 1	Timed Drill 2	Warm-up 2	Timed Drill 3	Timed Drill 4	Warm-up 3	Timed Drill 5	Timed Drill 6	Warm-up 4	Timed Drill 7	Timed Drill 8	Warm-up 5	Timed Drill 9	Warm-up 6	Timed Drill 10	Timed Drill 11	Review A	Review B	Review C
GOAL 1: Problem Solving — build new mathematical knowledge through problem solving; solve problems that arise in mathematics and in other contexts; apply and adapt a variety of appropriate strategies to solve problems; monitor and reflect on the process of mathematical problem solving.	✓	✓	✓	✓	✓	✓	✓	✓	✓	✓	✓	✓	✓	✓	✓	✓	✓	✓	✓	✓
GOAL 2: Reasoning & Proof — recognize reasoning and proof as fundamental aspects of mathematics; make and investigate mathematical conjectures; develop and evaluate mathematical arguments and proofs; select and use various types of reasoning and methods of proof.	✓	✓	✓	✓	✓	✓	✓	✓	✓	✓	✓	✓	✓	✓	✓	✓	✓	✓	✓	✓
GOAL 3: Communication — organize and consolidate their mathematical thinking through communication; communicate their mathematical thinking coherently and clearly to peers, teachers, and others; analyze and evaluate the mathematical thinking and strategies of others; use the language of mathematics to express mathematical ideas precisely.	✓	✓	✓	✓	✓	✓	✓	✓	✓	✓	✓	✓	✓	✓	✓	✓	✓	✓	✓	✓
GOAL 4: Connections — recognize and use connections among mathematical ideas; understand how mathematical ideas interconnect and build on one another to produce a coherent whole; recognize and apply mathematics in contexts outside of mathematics.	✓	✓	✓	✓	✓	✓	✓	✓	✓	✓	✓	✓	✓	✓	✓	✓	✓	✓	✓	✓
GOAL 5: Representation — create and use representations to organize, record, and communicate mathematical ideas; select, apply, and translate among mathematical representations to solve problems; use representations to model and interpret physical, social, and mathematical phenomena.	✓	✓	✓	✓	✓	✓	✓	✓	✓	✓	✓	✓	✓	✓	✓	✓	✓	✓	✓	✓

Expectations

Instructional programs from pre-kindergarten through grade 12 should enable all students to:

Contents

✔ **6 BONUS** Activity Pages! **Additional worksheets for your students**
✔ **3 BONUS** Overhead Transparencies! **For use with your**
projection system or interactive whiteboard

FREE!

- Go to our website: **www.classroomcompletepress.com/bonus**
- Enter item CC3116
- Enter pass code CC3116D for Activity Pages. CC3116A for Overheads.

Contents

✔ **6 BONUS Activity Pages!** Additional worksheets for your students
✔ **3 BONUS Overhead Transparencies!** For use with your projection system or interactive whiteboard

FREE!

- Go to our website: **www.classroomcompletepress.com/bonus**
- Enter item CC3216
- Enter pass code CC3216D for Activity Pages. CC3216A for Overheads.

NCTM Content Standards Assessment Rubric

Data Analysis & Probability – Task & Drill Sheets

Student's Name: _____   Assignment: _____   Level: _____

	Level 1	Level 2	Level 3	Level 4
Formulate questions that can be addressed with data and collect, organize, and display relevant data to answer them	• Demonstrates a limited ability to formulate questions that can be addressed with data and collect, organize, and display relevant data to answer them	• Demonstrates a basic ability to formulate questions that can be addressed with data and collect, organize, and display relevant data to answer them	• Demonstrates a good ability to formulate questions that can be addressed with data and collect, organize, and display relevant data to answer them	• Demonstrates a thorough ability to formulate questions that can be addressed with data and collect, organize, and display relevant data to answer them
Select and use appropriate statistical methods to analyze data	• Demonstrates a limited ability to select and use appropriate statistical methods to analyze data	• Demonstrates a basic ability to select and use appropriate statistical methods to analyze data	• Demonstrates a good ability to select and use appropriate statistical methods to analyze data	• Demonstrates a thorough ability to select and use appropriate statistical methods to analyze data
Develop and evaluate inferences and predictions that are based on data	• Demonstrates a limited ability to develop and evaluate inferences and predictions that are based on data	• Demonstrates a basic ability to develop and evaluate inferences and predictions that are based on data	• Demonstrates a good ability to develop and evaluate inferences and predictions that are based on data	• Demonstrates a thorough ability to develop and evaluate inferences and predictions that are based on data

STRENGTHS:

WEAKNESSES:

NEXT STEPS:

Before You Teach

Teacher Guide

Our resource has been created for ease of use by both TEACHERS and STUDENTS alike.

Introduction

The NCTM content standards have been used in the creation of the assignments in this booklet. This method promotes the idea that it is beneficial to learn through practical, applicable, real-world examples. Many of the task and drill sheets are organized around a central problem taken from real-life experiences of the students. The pages of this booklet contain a variety in terms of levels of difficulty and content so as to provide students with a variety of different opportunities. Included in our resource are activities to help students learn how to collect, organize, analyze, interpret, and predict data probabilities. Visual models are included to assist visual learners. Teachers may also choose to use mathematics manipulatives along with the exercises included in this book to help address the needs of kinesthetic learners.

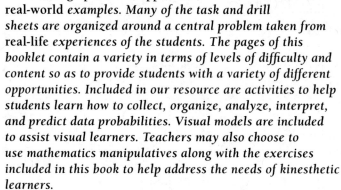

How Is Our Resource Organized?

STUDENT HANDOUTS

Reproducible **task sheets** and **drill sheets** make up the majority of our resource.

The **task sheets** contain challenging problem-solving tasks in drill form, many centered around 'real-world' ideas or problems, which push the boundaries of critical thought and demonstrate to students why mathematics is important and applicable in the real world. It is not expected that all activities will be used, but are offered for variety and flexibility in teaching and assessment. Many of the drill sheet problems offer space for reflection, and opportunity for the appropriate use of technology, as encouraged by the NCTM's *Principles & Standards for School Mathematics*.

The **drill sheets** contain 11 Timed Drill Sheets and 6 Warm-Up Drill Sheets, featuring real-life problem-solving opportunities. The drill sheets are provided to help students with their procedural proficiency skills, as emphasized by the *NCTM's Curriculum Focal Points*.

The **NCTM Content Standards Assessment Rubric** (*page 6*) is a useful tool for evaluating students' work in many of the activities in our resource. The **Reviews** (*pages 26-28 and 46-48*) are divided by grade and can be used for a follow-up review or assessment at the completion of the unit.

PICTURE CUES

Our resource contains three main types of pages, each with a different purpose and use. A **Picture Cue** at the top of each page shows, at a glance, what the page is for.

 Teacher Guide

* Information and tools for the teacher

 Student Handout

* Reproducible drill sheets

 Easy Marking™ Answer Key

* Answers for student activities

 Timed Drill Stopwatch

* Write the amount of time for students to complete the timed drill sheet in the stopwatch. Recommended times are given on the contents page.

EASY MARKING™ ANSWER KEY

Marking students' worksheets is fast and easy with our **Answer Key**. Answers are listed in columns – just line up the column with its corresponding worksheet, as shown, and see how every question matches up with its answer!

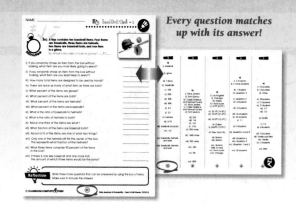

Every question matches up with its answer!

Principles & Standards

Principles & Standards for School Mathematics outlines the essential components of an effective school mathematics program.

The NCTM's Principles & Standards for School Mathematics

The **Principles** are the fundamentals to an effective mathematics education. The **Standards** are descriptions of what mathematics instruction should enable students to learn. Together the **Principles and Standards** offer a comprehensive and coherent set of learning goals, serving as a resource to teachers and a framework for curriculum. Our resource offers exercises written to the NCTM **Process** and **Content Standards** and is inspired by the **Principles** outlined below.

Six Principles for School Mathematics

Equity

Curriculum

Teaching

Learning

Assessment

Technology

EQUITY: All students can learn mathematics when they have access to high-quality instruction, including reasonable and appropriate accommodation and appropriately challenging content.

CURRICULUM: The curriculum must be coherent, focused, and well articulated across the grades, with ideas linked to and building on one another to deepen students' knowledge and understanding.

TEACHING: Effective teaching requires understanding what students know and need to learn and then challenging and supporting them to learn it well.

LEARNING: By aligning factual knowledge and procedural proficiency with conceptual knowledge, students can become effective learners, reflecting on their thinking and learning from their mistakes.

ASSESSMENT: The tasks teachers select for assessment convey a message to students about what kinds of knowledge and performance are valued. Feedback promotes goal-setting, responsibility, and independence.

TECHNOLOGY: Students can develop a deeper understanding of mathematics with the appropriate use of technology, which can allow them to focus on decision-making, reflection, reasoning, and problem solving.

Our resource correlates to the six Principles and provides teachers with supplementary materials, which can aid them in fulfilling the expectations of each principle. The exercises provided allow for variety and flexibility in teaching and assessment. The topical division of concepts and processes promotes linkage and the building of conceptual knowledge and understanding throughout the student's grade and middle school career. Each of the drill sheet problems help students with their procedural proficiency skills, and offers space for reflection and opportunity for the appropriate use of technology.

NAME: _____

Task Sheet 1

1) Central tendency is the measure of the middle number in a group of numbers. The mean is the sum of a set of numbers divided by the amount of numbers in a set. The mode is the value that occurs most often.

a) **Here are the weekly fundraising amounts for the students in Fred's class.**

Week 1 .... $73.45
Week 2 .... $16.47
Week 3 .... $8.64
Week 4 .... $10.92
Week 5 .... $51.00

i) What is the mean fundraising amount?

ii) What is the mode fundraising amount?

iii) What if Fred brings in 51 dollars more. What are the mean and mode?

b) **Find the mean for each set of numbers.**

i) 6,7,7,5

ii) 2,8,9,8,4

iii) 3,1,4,6,6,5

c) **Find the mode for each set of numbers in question b).**

i) 6,7,7,5

ii) 2,8,9,8,4

iii) 3,1,4,6,6,5

NAME: _____

Task Sheet 2

2) Roman and Sofia grew grapes on 325 acres. Boris and Elvira also grew grapes, but only had 205 acres. Catarina and Marcos grew the fewest number of grapes on 85 acres of land.

a) **Create a pictograph with a title, a key, and include all the information above in your graph.**

Key

b) **Write two observations about your graph once it is complete.**

_____

_____

c) **Write two questions that can be answered from the data in the graph.**

_____

_____

Task Sheet 3

3) Central tendency is the measure of the middle number in a group of numbers. The median is the middle value of a list or group of numbers, in numerical order. The range is the difference between the highest and the lowest numbers.

a) Jarod's hockey team scored the following number of goals in their last 7 playoff games.

4,6,5,3,2,2,1

i)   What is the median for the set of numbers above?

ii)   What does the median tell you about the goals scored?

_____

_____

iii)   What is the range for the set of numbers above?

iv)   What does the range tell you about the goals scored?

_____

_____

b) Give an example of when the range would be the most accurate measurement for finding the central tendency in a group of numbers?

_____

_____

c) Give an example for when the median would be the most accurate measurement for finding the central tendency in a group of numbers?

_____

_____

Task Sheet 4

4) Ask 30 people what their favorite car is. In the circle graph below, display the data you collected.

Express your answers in a ratio and a percent.

	Ratio	**Percent**
a) How many people chose a domestically made car?		
b) How many chose a foreign made car?		
c) How many were sports cars?		

d) Create three questions of your own that can be answered by the data in the graph.

_____

_____

_____

_____

Task Sheet 5

5) Olaf, Marta, Freya, and Rolf, tossed their coins in the air 15 times each. They recorded the number of times they got heads and tails.

Person	Heads	Tails
Olaf	10	5
Marta	6	9
Freya	3	12
Rolf	13	2

a) What patterns do you see in the data in the table?

_____

_____

b) What inferences can you make about the data in the table?

_____

_____

c) What two questions can you ask that can be answered by the data in the table?

_____

_____

d) If all four people flipped their coin 5 more times, what would the probability be for the difference between the number of times heads and tails were chosen to remain the same?

_____

_____

_____

_____

NAME: _____

Task Sheet 6

6) Create four sets of numbers.

The first set of numbers will have a mode of 12.

The second set of numbers will have a median of 36.

The third set of numbers will have a mean of 17.

The fourth set of numbers will have a range of 24.

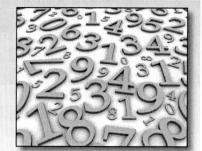

a)

b)

c)

d)

Reflection Explain the strategies you used to determine each set of numbers.

Data Analysis & Probability – Task & Drill Sheets CC3316

Task Sheet 7

7) Complete the number of stripes on a zebra frequency table.

Recorded data:

2, 4, 6, 6, 18, 22, 14, 10, 16, 20, 6, 20, 12, 12, 18, 16, 6, 20

Stripes	2	4	6	10	12	14	16	18	20	22
Frequency										

a) **What is the median?**

b) **What is the mode?**

c) **What is the mean?**

d) **What is the range?**

e) **What other data can you observe from the table?**

_____

_____

_____

_____

_____

_____

_____

_____

Task Sheet 8

NAME: _____

8) Finish labeling the graph below. Then, find the coordinates for the apples and write them into the designated spaces provided.

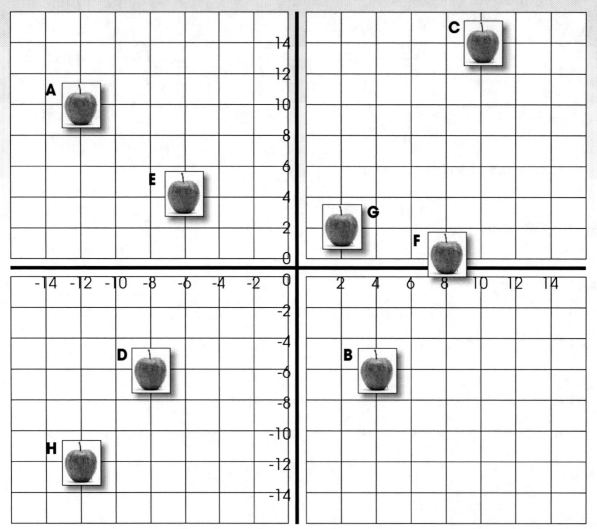

a)

b)

c)

d)

e)

f)

g)

h)

Data Analysis & Probability – Task & Drill Sheets CC3316

NAME: _____

Task Sheet 9

9) Finish labeling the graph below. Then, find the coordinates for the vertices shown in the designated space provided. Remember, a vertex is a node in a graph.

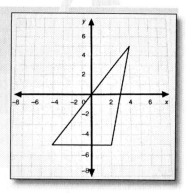

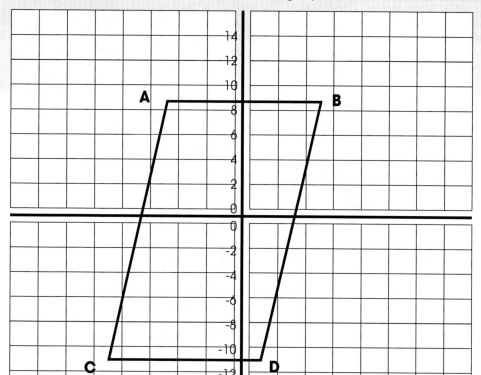

a) [ ]

b) [ ]

c) [ ]

d) [ ]

Reflection Name the shape shown in the graph above. List the properties of the shape shown.

NAME: _____

Task Sheet 10

10) Graph the following coordinates on the grid. Show each coordinate with a star.

a) 0, -15	**b)** 6, 12
c) -9, 9	**d)** 21, 21
e) -3, 15	**f)** -18, -12

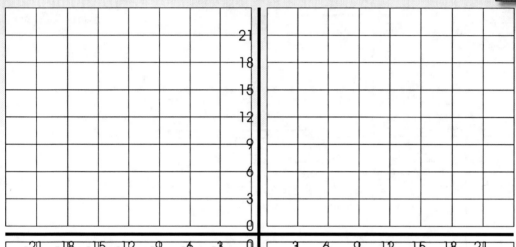

Reflection What patterns do you see in the coordinates? Explain.

_____

_____

Task Sheet 11

11) The following are the Top Ten most visited Internet sites.

    1)   Yahoo Sites
    2)   Time Warner Network
    3)   Microsoft Sites
    4)   Google Sites
    5)   eBay
    6)   Fox Interactive Media
    7)   Amazon Sites
    8)   Ask Network
    9)   Wikipedia Sites
    10)   New York Times Digital

a) **Represent this information in the circle graph provided below.**

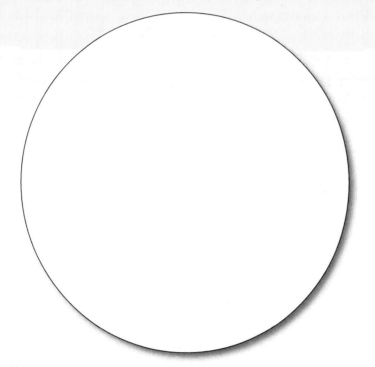

Explore With Technology

Visit http://searchengineland.com/wikipedia-enters-top-ten-most-visited-sites-10536 to see how many millions of visitors each site had and input this information in a graph other than a circle graph.

Task Sheet

NAME: _____

Task Sheet 12

12) The following teams belong to the Northeast Division of the NHL.

Boston Bruins, Buffalo Sabres, Montreal Canadians, Ottawa Senators, and the Toronto Maple Leafs.

Using the list above, answer the following questions with a fraction.

a) What is the probability that the Boston Bruins will win the Stanley Cup?

b) What is the probability that the Buffalo Sabres will win the Stanley Cup?

c) What is the probability that the Montréal Canadians will win the Stanley Cup?

d) What is the probability that the Ottawa Senators will win the Stanley Cup?

e) What is the probability that the Toronto Maple Leafs will win the Stanley Cup?

f) What is the probability of a Canadian team winning the Stanley Cup?

g) What is the probability of an American team winning the Stanley Cup?

h) Create a graph that expresses the probabilities of a) – g) in percentages.

© CLASSROOM COMPLETE PRESS

Data Analysis & Probability – Task & Drill Sheets CC3316

Task Sheet 13

13) Damario, Elonzo, Felippe, and Victorio all took shots on the goal for the men's soccer team. They made their shots from:

9, 12, 2, 5, 9, 14, 3, 3, 1, 4, 9, 3, 6, 8, 7, 3 feet.

Kalle, Akira, Sabre, and Lanelle took shots on the goal for the women's soccer team. They made their shots from:

14, 12, 9, 5, 5, 4, 2, 1, 12, 5, 3, 6, 8, 9, 5, 4 feet.

Label and plot these distances in a Scatter plot graph below for the men and the women. Use circles for the men and triangles for the women. Then, answer the questions below.

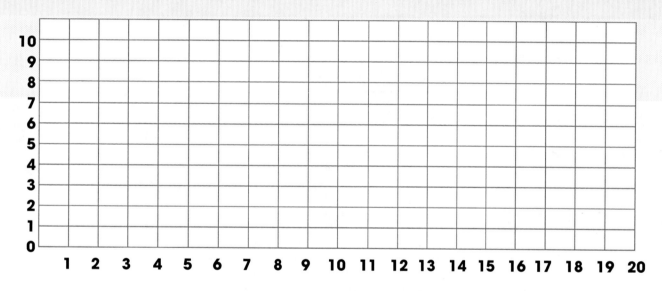

a) How many shots were taken 4 feet from the goal?

b) How many players made the shot 9 feet from the goal?

c) Is there a correlation between the shots made and the distance from the goal?

d) Is the correlation weak or strong?

e) Is the correlation positive or negative?

Task Sheet 14

14) Flip a coin 40 times with a partner. Record the outcome in the tally chart below, then label and plot the data on the bar graph provided. Use one color to distinguish heads, and another for tails.

	Outcome	
	Heads	**Tails**
Person A		
Person B		

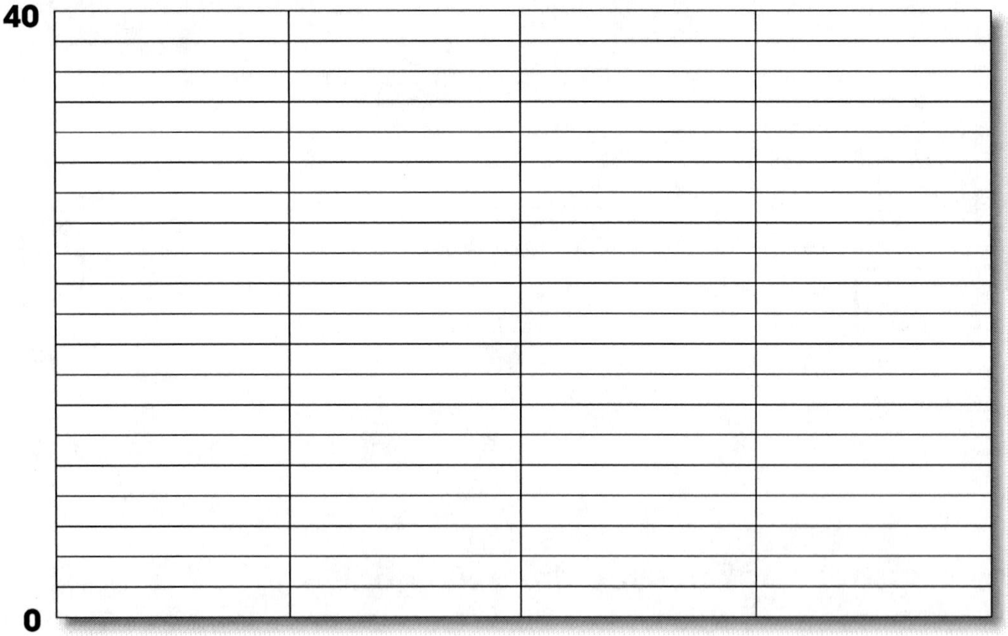

40

0

Reflection — **Indicate the probability of flipping heads or tails for each person and as a whole.**

_____

_____

Task Sheet 15

15) Roxanne, Isaac, Lonny, and Abigail went to the mall to buy shoes.

These are the shoe sizes that were available in the store they went to:

6, 5, 2, 8, 8.5, 6, 7.5, 4, 9, 8, 2, 4, 6.5, 8, 10, 12

a) **Find the mean.**

b) **Find the mode.**

c) **Find the median.**

d) **Find the range.**

Survey your class for their shoe sizes. Group your findings into boys and girls. Express your answers in percentages.

e) **What is the probability that the girls would find their shoe size?**

f) **What is the probability that the boys will find their shoe size?**

g) **What is the probability the entire class will find their shoe size?**

h) **What is the probability of you finding your shoe size?**

Explore With Technology

Go to http://www.sears.ca/gp/home.html and click on shoes. Graph the types of shoes that are on sale.

NAME: _____

Drill Sheet 1

Choose the best answer for each question.

a) Presents pieces of data in a format for comparison.

   i)   Bar Graph
   ii) Circle Graph
   iii) Pictograph
   iv) Line Graph
   v)   Double Bar Graph
   vi) Histogram
   vii) Scatter Plot

b) Shows parts of a whole in percentages.

   i)   Circle Graph
   ii) Double Bar Graph
   iii) Pictograph
   iv) Scatter Plot
   v)   Histogram
   vi) Bar Graph
   vii) Line Graph

c) Data in varying intervals are compared.

   i)   Scatter Plot
   ii) Bar Graph
   iii) Histogram
   iv) Circle Graph
   v)   Pictograph
   vi) Line Graph
   vii) Double Bar Graph

d) Shows information over a period of time.

   i)   Bar Graph
   ii) Circle Graph
   iii) Line Graph
   iv) Pictograph
   v)   Histogram
   vi) Double Bar Graph
   vii) Scatter Plot

e) Comparing data in numerical groupings.

   i)   Circle Graph
   ii) Histogram
   iii) Line Graph
   iv) Bar Graph
   v)   Double Bar Graph
   vi) Scatter Plot
   vii) Pictograph

f) Uses symbols to represent and compare information.

   i)   Bar Graph
   ii) Scatter Plot
   iii) Double Bar Graph
   iv) Histogram
   v)   Pictograph
   vi) Circle Graph
   vii) Line Graph

NAME: _____

Drill Sheet 2

An outlier is a number that is significantly different from the rest of the grouping of numbers.

The following goals were scored at a basketball game.

The goals were scored at 1:56, 2:18, 2:35, 3:19, 4:12, 4:48, 1:56, 3:22, and 12:23.

a) **What is the mode?**

b) **What is the median?**

c) **What is the range?**

d) **What is the mean?**

e) **Which time is the outlier?**

f) **Calculate the mean, median, range, and mode without the outlier.**

Mean

Median

Mode

Range

g) **Explain how excluding the outlier changes the data. Is it a significant change. Why or why not?**

_____

_____

h) **How can you explain the outlier?**

_____

_____

Review A

Palmer has a bag of marbles. He has 20 marbles in his bag. He has 12 red marbles, 6 orange marbles, and 2 yellow marbles.

Show the probability of choosing each marble in fractions and percentages.

		Fraction	Percent
a)	**Choosing a red marble.**		
b)	**Choosing an orange marble.**		
c)	**Choosing a yellow marble.**		
d)	**Choosing an orange or yellow marble.**		

e) **What other questions can you ask and show as a fraction or percent for the marbles in Palmer's bag?**

_____

_____

_____

_____

_____

Reflection Express the mean, median, mode, and range for the marbles in Palmer's bag. Are these findings significant? Explain.

NAME: _____

Review B

Use the circle graph to answer the questions below.

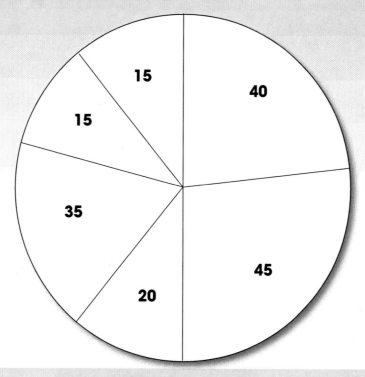

a)   **What does the information on the graph provide?**

_____

_____

b)   **What information is missing on the graph?**

_____

_____

c)   **Is the information provided on the graph correct? Explain.**

_____

_____

d)   **Recreate the graph on a separate piece of paper to make it more informative.**

Review C

All 260 students at Pamela's school were surveyed on their favorite type of snack.
The results were:

Chips	55
Cookies	25
Granola Bars	16
Fruit	39
Yogurt	16
Candy	42
Chocolate	67

On a separate piece of paper, show this information in two different types of graphs.
Answer the following questions for both graphs.

a) **What two graphs did you choose to represent the information above and why?**

_____

_____

b) **Which snack was chosen the most? The least?**

_____

c) **What inferences can you make from the information gathered in the survey?**

_____

d) **What percentage of students chose yogurt and fruit for their snack?**

_____

Explore With Technology

Visit http://www.hc-sc.gc.ca/fn-an/food-guide-aliment/index-eng.php. Use the food guide to graph the food choices by the students for their snacks. Create your own food guide and assess the data you input in percentage and ratio form.

NAME: _____

1a) **The triple bar chart below shows the results of a survey done with students in three classrooms. The students were asked which pie flavor is their favorite.**

Ex: How many students are there in all 3 classes? ___59___

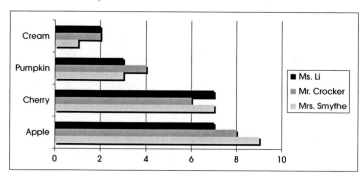

i) How many students are in Ms. Li's class? _____

ii) How many students are in Mr. Crocker's class? _____

iii) How many students are in Mrs. Smythe's class? _____

iv) How many students in Mrs. Smythe's class like pumpkin pie best? _____

v) How many students in Mr. Crocker's class like cherry pie best? _____

vi) How many students in Ms. Li's class did not select cream pie as a favorite? _____

vii) Which two classes had two students who liked cream pie? _____

viii) How many more students in Mrs. Smythe's class liked apple pie than cherry pie? _____

ix) Three students in Ms. Li's class liked what type of pie? _____

x) How many more students in Mrs. Smythe's class liked apple pie than students who liked apple pie in Ms. Li's class? _____

xi) How many more students in Mr. Crocker's class liked pumpkin pie than cream pie? _____

xii) How many students in Mrs. Smythe's class liked cherry or pumpkin pie? _____

xiii) The same amount of students in what two classrooms liked cherry pie? _____

xiv) The most popular pie in all three classes was what flavor? _____

xv) The least popular pie in all three classes was what flavor? _____

xvi) What was the average number of students who voted for apple pie as their favorite? _____

Reflection Conduct your own survey in your class about favorite desserts. Make a graph to show your results.

Timed Drill Sheet # 1   NAME: _____

2a) **The following table shows the results of the Carroll Middle School 5 mile (8 km) Road Race.**
Ex: What is the mode of Jessica, Miguel, Carla and Leigh's race times? <u>28.15 min</u>

Road Race results (in minutes and hundredths of a minute)

Jessica's time = 28.15 min	Arthur's time = 27.40 min	Dominic's time = 27.50 min
Miguel's time = 27.45 min	Chelsea's time = 29.01 min	Ariel's time = 27.55 min
Carla's time = 29.23 min	Leigh's time = 28.15 min	Ella's time = 29.03 min
Won's time = 28.67 min	Tim's time = 27.63 min	Tia's time = 27.83 min

i) Who had the fastest time in this group? _____

ii) Who had the slowest time in this group? _____

iii) What is the range of times in this group? _____

iv) What was Dominic's average time per mile (km)? _____

v) What was Leigh's average time per mile (km)? _____

vi) How much faster was Won than Chelsea? _____

vii) What was the average time of Miguel, Dominic, and Arthur? _____

viii) What was the mode of the race times? _____

ix) How much slower was Jessica than Miguel? _____

x) What was the average time of Miguel and Tim? _____

xi) Who was 1.08 minutes faster than Carla? _____

xii) Who was five hundredths of a minute slower than Dominic? _____

xiii) How much faster was Tim than Tia? _____

xiv) Which student came in second place in these results? _____

xv) Which student came in fifth place in these results? _____

xvi) Who was 0.02 minutes faster than Ella? _____

Explore With Technology

Use a graphing program online or on your computer to graph the results of this race.

NAME: _____

Minutes

3a) **A box contains ten baseball items. Four items are baseballs, three items are helmets, two items are baseball bats, and one item is a glove.**

Ex: What is the ratio of bats to gloves? ___2:1___

i) If you randomly chose an item from the box without looking, what item are you most likely going to select?

_____

ii) If you randomly chose an item from the box without looking, what item are you least likely to select?

_____

iii) How many total items are designed to be used by hands?

_____

iv) There are twice as many of what item as there are bats?

_____

v) What percent of the items are gloves?

_____

vi) What percent of the items are bats?

_____

vii) What percent of the items are helmets?

_____

viii) What percent of the items are baseballs?

_____

ix) What is the ratio of baseballs to helmets?

_____

x) What is the ratio of helmets to bats?

_____

xi) About one-third of the items are what?

_____

xii) What fraction of the items are baseball bats?

_____

xiii) About 6/10 of the items are one of what two things?

_____

xiv) Only one of the helmets still fits the owner of the box. This represents what fraction of the helmets?

_____

xv) What three items comprise 90 percent of the items in the box?

_____

xvi) If there is one less baseball and one more bat, the amount of which three items would be the same?

_____

Reflection

Write three more questions that can be answered by using this box of items. Make sure to include the answers.

4a) **The pie chart below represents the percent of votes four candidates received in a mayor's race.**

Ex: If 3,600 people voted, how many votes did Caleb Wallace and Samuel Owens receive?   3,600 x 0.5 (50%) = <u>1800 votes</u>

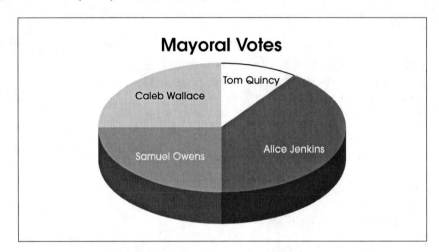

i) Which candidate won the mayoral race?   _____

ii) Which candidate came in last?   _____

iii) What two candidates tied in the race?   _____

iv) Who received about 40 percent of the vote?   _____

v) Alice Jenkins received a little under twice as many votes
   as which two candidates?   _____

vi) Which candidate received one-fifth of the vote that Alice
    Jenkins received?   _____

vii) What fraction of the vote did Alice Jenkins receive?   _____

viii) What fraction of the vote did Samuel Owens receive?   _____

ix) What fraction of the vote did Caleb Wallace receive?   _____

x) What fraction of the vote did Tom Quincy receive?   _____

xi) If 3,600 people voted, how many votes did Caleb Wallace
    receive?   _____

xii) If 3,600 people voted, how many votes did Alice Jenkins
     receive?   _____

xiii) If 3,600 people voted, how many votes did Samuel Owens
      receive?   _____

xiv) If 3,600 people voted, how many votes did Tom Quincy
     receive?   _____

xv) The percent of votes Tom Quincy received in this election
    doubled from the previous election. What percent of the vote
    did he receive in the previous election?   _____

xvi) Alice Jenkins percent of the vote also doubled since the last
     election? If the trend continues, what percent of the vote will
     she receive in the next election?

NAME: _____

Timed Drill Sheet # 3

Minutes

5a) The climate chart below shows the data for seven cities compiled by The Weather Network.

City	Monthly Average Temperature				Annual Precipitation	Annual Snowfall
	January	April	July	October		
Boston	29.3°F (–1.5°C)	48.3°F (9.1°C)	73.9°F (23.3°C)	54.1°F (12.3°C)	42.53 in (1080 mm)	42.80 in (108.71 cm)
Mexico City	55.4°F (13.0°C)	64.4°F (18.0°C)	60.8°F (16.0°C)	60.8°F (16.0°C)	33.39 in (848 mm)	0 in (0 cm)
Chicago	22.0°F (–5.6°C)	47.8°F (8.8°C)	73.3°F (22.9°C)	52.1°F (11.2°C)	36.27 in (921.26 mm)	38.00 in (96.52 cm)
Dallas	44.1°F (6.7°C)	65.0°F (18.3°C)	85.0°F (29.4°C)	67.2°F (19.6°C)	34.73 in (882.14 mm)	2.60 in (6.60 cm)
Vancouver	40.6°F (4.8°C)	50.0°F (10.0°C)	64.6°F (18.1°C)	52.0°F (11.1°C)	58.11 in (1476 mm)	17.32 in (44 cm)
Los Angeles	57.1°F (13.9°C)	60.8°F (16.0°C)	69.3°F (20.7°C)	66.9°F (19.4°C)	13.15 in (334 mm)	0 in (0 cm)
New York City	32.1°F (0.1°C)	52.5°F (11.4°C)	76.5°F (24.7°C)	56.6°F (13.7°C)	49.69 in (1262.13 mm)	28.60 in (72.64 cm)

i) Which city has the warmest average January temperature? _____

ii) Which city has the coldest average January temperature? _____

iii) Which city has the warmest average April temperature? _____

iv) Which city has the coldest average October temperature? _____

v) How much warmer is the average October temperature of Dallas than Los Angeles? _____

vi) What is the range of January average temperatures? _____

vii) What is the average combined temperatures of Boston, Chicago, and Vancouver in July? _____

viii) What is the average combined temperature of Vancouver and Los Angeles in October? _____

ix) Which city had the highest average temperature for 3 months? _____

x) What is the average temperature of New York for the four months shown? _____

xi) Which city is 11.9°F (6.6°C) warmer on average in July than Vancouver? _____

xii) Which city has the highest annual snowfall? _____

xiii) Which city averages 4.8 more inches (12.19 cm) of snowfall per year than Chicago? _____

xiv) How much more annual precipitation does New York City have than Los Angeles? _____

xv) Which city has the highest annual precipitation? _____

xvi) Which city has a little more than 3 feet of annual precipitation per year? _____

Timed Drill Sheet # 4

NAME: _____

6a) **The line plot below shows the number of students who answered questions wrong on a math test in two of Mr. Gregorio's classes, class A and class B.**

Ex: One quarter of students in team B got question 5 incorrect. How many total students are in the class?   4 x 3 = <u>12 students</u>

X = 1 student

Q1 A	Q1 B	Q2 A	Q2 B	Q3 A	Q3 B	Q4 A	Q4 B	Q5 A	Q5 B	Q6 A	Q6 B	Q7 A	Q7 B	Q8 A	Q8 B	Q9 A	Q9 B
										X							
										X					X		
										X	X		X	X	X		
		X				X	X	X		X	X	X	X	X	X		
X		X				X	X	X	X	X	X	X	X	X	X		
X		X		X		X	X	X	X	X	X	X	X	X	X		
X	X	X	X	X	X	X	X	X	X	X	X	X	X	X	X	X	X
A	**B**	**A**	**B**	**A**	**B**	**A**	**B**	**A**	**B**	**A**	**B**	**A**	**B**	**A**	**B**	**A**	**B**
Question 1		Question 2		Question 3		Question 4		Question 5		Question 6		Question 7		Question 8		Question 9	

i) How many total students got question 1 wrong? _____

ii) How many more students in team B got question 7 wrong than in team A? _____

iii) How many total students in team A got question 9 wrong? _____

iv) Which question had the fewest students who got it wrong in both classes? _____

v) Which question did no one in team A get incorrect? _____

vi) What is the mode of numbers of students who get a question wrong? _____

vii) What was the average number of students who got question 4 wrong? _____

viii) How many total questions did team B get incorrect? _____

ix) How many total questions did team A get incorrect? _____

x) What is the ratio of number of questions that team A got wrong to the number of questions team B got wrong? _____

xi) How many more total student got question 6 wrong than question 5 wrong? _____

xii) Which two questions were answered incorrectly by three students on each team? _____

xiii) Which question was likely the most difficult to answer? _____

xiv) Which question was likely the easiest to answer? _____

xv) Which questions had twice as many members of team A answering them incorrectly than team B? _____

xvi) One fifth of the students in team A got question 5 incorrect? How many total students are in the class? _____

7a) The chart below shows the favorite ice cream flavors of a grade 6 and 7 class.

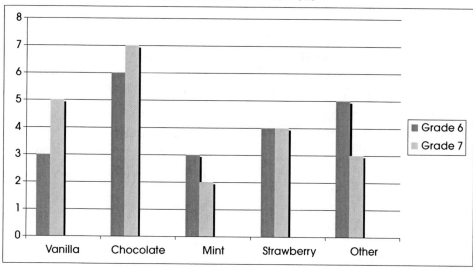

FAVORITE ICE CREAM FLAVORS

i) What was the most popular flavor with the grade 6 class? _____

ii) What was the most popular flavor with the grade 7 class? _____

iii) Suppose a student answered "Neapolitan". Which category would this be under? _____

iv) An equal amount of 6th graders and 7th graders selected what flavor? _____

v) How many total 6th graders were asked to take part in this poll? _____

vi) How many total 7th graders were asked to take part in this poll? _____

vii) What fraction of the total 6th graders chose mint as their favorite flavor? _____

viii) What fraction of the total 7th graders chose chocolate as their favorite flavor? _____

ix) Eight total students in both grades chose what two flavors as their favorites? _____

x) What is the ratio of 7th graders to 6th graders who like chocolate most? _____

xi) What is the average number of students who selected vanilla as their favorite flavor? _____

xii) Three less 7th grade students like strawberry than what flavor? _____

xiii) Half as many 6th graders like what flavor than chocolate? _____

xiv) A ratio of 5 to 3 students in grades 7 and 6 like what flavor? _____

xv) How many more students in both grades voted for chocolate than other? _____

xvi) Five total students liked what flavor? _____

Timed Drill Sheet # 5   NAME: _____

8a) The box scores chart below shows the statistics for one team during a college basketball game.

Ex: What is the average amount of rebounds? ___5___

Mudhens Box Score

Name	Minutes	Points	Rebounds	Assists
Allen, Paul	28	15	5	3
Bryant, Ray	25	16	3	2
Smith, Jake	26	10	8	1
Jones, Karl	28	9	6	2
Kidd, Greg	20	5	5	9
Drew, Dave	24	7	4	2
Rivera, Diego	20	8	5	0
Carter, Gabe	19	5	4	1

i) How many total players played in the game for the Mudhens? _____

ii) Which player played the least amount of minutes? _____

iii) What was the mode for minutes played? _____

iv) What was the average amount of minutes played by the players on the Mudhens? _____

v) Which player actually played the average amount of minutes? _____

vi) How many total points were scored by the Mudhens? _____

vii) What two players combined to score as many points as Jake Smith? _____

viii) One third of the points were scored by what three players? _____

ix) What is the ratio of Paul Allen's points to Jake Smith's points? _____

x) Which player had an equal amount of points and rebounds? _____

xi) How many total rebounds did the team have? _____

xii) What was the mode for rebounds? _____

xiii) Which player had one-fifth of the rebounds? _____

xiv) What was the range in assists for the Mudhens? _____

xv) Greg Kidd had three times as many assists as what player? _____

xvi) What is the average amount of assists? _____

9a) **The thermograph sheet below shows how temperature changed during a six hour period for two days.**

Ex: What is the pattern in temperature drop on Friday between 10:00 pm and 12:00 am?   Drops 3°F (2°C) each hour

Nighttime Temperatures

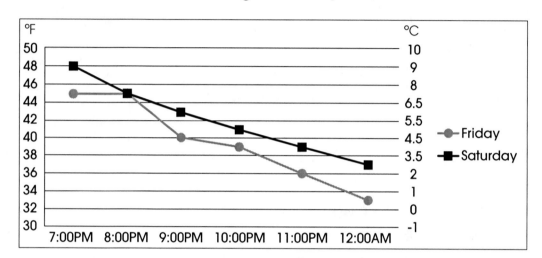

i) Which day had the warmest temperature between 7:00 PM and 12:00 AM?   _____

ii) Which day had the coldest temperature between 7:00 PM and 12:00 AM?   _____

iii) What temperature was recorded at 9:00 PM on Friday?   _____

iv) What temperature was recorded at 11:00 PM on Saturday?   _____

v) What time on both days was the same temperature recorded?   _____

vi) The temperature on Friday at 10:00 PM was the same as the temperature on Saturday at what time?   _____

vii) How much did the temperature drop on Friday from 7:00 PM to 12:00 AM?   _____

viii) How much did the temperature drop on Saturday from 7:00 PM to 12:00 AM?   _____

ix) What was the average drop between the two days?   _____

x) On which day did the temperature dip to 36°F (2°C)?   _____

xi) What was the difference in temperature at 10:00 PM between Saturday and Friday?   _____

xii) The biggest drop in temperature on Friday happened between what hours?   _____

xiii) The biggest drop in temperature on Saturday happened between what hours?   _____

xiv) Which day saw the temperature go closest to the freezing point?   _____

xv) On Saturday between 7:00 PM and 10:00 PM, the temperature dropped how many degrees?   _____

xvi) What is the pattern in temperature drop on Saturday between 8:00 PM and 12:00 AM?   _____

10a) The following tally chart shows the results of a class president election.

Ex: Sixteen percent of the vote went to which student? ___Won___

Name	Number of Votes		
Carmen	/////	//	
Won	/////	////	
Jessica	/////	/////	/////
Michael	/////	/////	/
Antoine	/////	/////	///

i) Which student received the most votes? _____

ii) Which student received the least amount of votes? _____

iii) How many total votes were tallied? _____

iv) One-eighth of the total votes went to which student? _____

v) Twenty percent of the vote went to which student? _____

vi) Which student received two less votes than Jessica? _____

vii) Which two students combined had one more vote than Jessica? _____

viii) What was the average amount of votes received by the students? _____

ix) Which students received more than the average amount of votes? _____

x) Which student received the average amount of votes? _____

xi) Which students received less than the average amount of votes? _____

xii) Antoine received four more votes than which student? _____

xiii) What is the range of votes received? _____

xiv) Students were most likely to vote for which student? _____

xv) How many votes were not received by Michael? _____

xvi) What is the ratio of votes received by Won to votes received by Jessica? _____

Reflection

Explain what type of graph would best show the data from this table above. Why would you use this graph? Then, complete the graph with the information above.

NAME: _____

Timed Drill Sheet # 7

Minutes

11a) Sports Centre is having its annual Winter Blast Sale on sports items. The following chart below shows the pre and post sale prices.

Ex: Which sale item cost one eighth of one other item pre sale?   Baseballs cost 1/8 of hockey gloves

Item	Pre sale price	Post sale price
Hockey stick	$80.00	$72.00
Hockey gloves	$56.00	$50.00
Basketball hoop	$50.00	$40.00
Basketball sneakers	$80.00	$68.00
Basketballs	$12.00	$9.00
Baseball bats	$25.00	$22.00
Baseball helmets	$40.00	$35.00
Baseballs	$8.00	$7.00
Footballs	$26.00	$22.00

i) Which items were the most expensive pre sale? _____
ii) Which item was the least expensive pre sale? _____
iii) Which item decreased in price by $6.00 for the sale? _____
iv) Which item decreased by the least amount of money for the sale? _____
v) Which item had a 10 percent discount for the sale? _____
vi) Which post sale items cost the same as other pre sale items? _____
vii) What item had exactly a 15 percent discount for the sale? _____
viii) What item has the largest percentage discount post sale? _____
ix) What two items cost the same post sale? _____
x) What items can be purchased for exactly $42.00 post sale? _____
xi) Which items could be purchased for a total of $37 pre sale? _____
xii) Which sale item cost one tenth of two other items pre sale? _____
xiii) What item cost $31 more than basketballs post sale? _____
xiv) What is the ratio of the price of hockey gloves to basketball hoops post sale? _____
xv) What is the mode of the post sale prices? _____
xvi) What is the range of the post sale prices? _____

Explore With Technology

Use your computer or internet to research the prices of the above sports equipment in your area. Write the prices and compare the costs of the items. Explain how the costs are similar and different.

Data Analysis & Probability – Task & Drill Sheets CC3316

© CLASSROOM COMPLETE PRESS

12a) The Museum of Science for Children has the following game in its probability room. Students press a button releasing a disc. The disc falls on one of the numbers on the game board below.

Ex: What is the probability that you will land on the number 5? __1 in 10__

1	2	3	4	5
6	7	8	9	10

i) What is the probability that you will land on an odd number?   _____

ii) What is the probability that you will land on an even number?   _____

iii) What is the ratio of odd numbers to even numbers?   _____

iv) What percent of the game board is made of white squares?   _____

v) What percent of the game board is made of light gray squares?   _____

vi) What fraction of the game board is made of dark gray squares?   _____

vii) What fraction of the squares have black numbers?   _____

viii) What fraction of the squares have white numbers?   _____

ix) What is the ratio of white numbers to black numbers?   _____

x) What percent of the numbers on the board are even and less than 10?   _____

xi) What are your chances of landing on a light gray square?   _____

xii) What are your chances of landing on a dark gray square with an odd number?   _____

xiii) What are your chances of landing on a white square with an odd number?   _____

xiv) What are your chances of landing on a light gray square with an odd number?   _____

xv) What are you more likely to land on, a dark gray square with an even number or a white square with an odd number?   _____

xvi) What are you more likely to land on, a dark gray square with an odd number, a light gray square with an odd number, or a square with white letters?   _____

Reflection   Create your own game board like this one. Write six probability statements using your board.

13a) **The graph below shows the number of snacks sold at the Brown Middle School snack shop during the past week.**

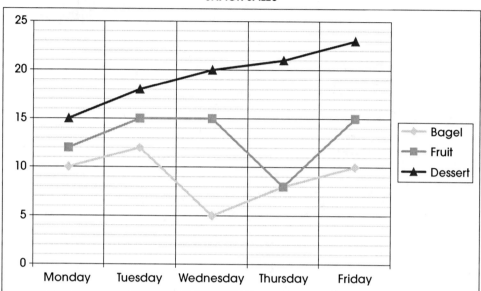

SNACK SALES

i) How many total desserts were sold during the week? _____

ii) How many pieces of fruit were sold during the week? _____

iii) How many total bagels were sold during the week? _____

iv) On which days were the least amount of snacks sold? _____

v) On which day were the most amount of snacks sold? _____

vi) On which day were 12 bagels sold? _____

vii) On which day were 12 pieces of fruit sold? _____

viii) On which two days were a total of 38 desserts sold? _____

ix) On what day was 25 bagels and pieces of fruit sold? _____

x) Which snack item increased in sales each day? _____

xi) Which snacks saw a sales decrease by seven items from one day to the next? _____

xii) What was the mode of sales for fruit? _____

xiii) On which day was the sale of bagels the same as the sale of fruit? _____

xiv) What was the average amount of desserts sold on a given day? _____

xv) The largest difference between the sale of desserts and the sale of bagels occurred on which day? _____

xvi) On which two consecutive days did the sale of a snack remain the same? _____

14a) The following bar graph shows the number of students who have birthdays during summer months in grades 7 and 8.

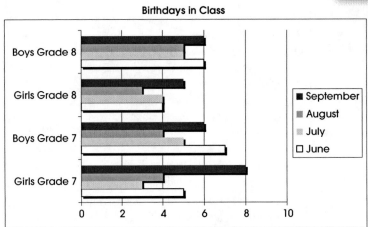

Birthdays in Class

i) How many total 7th grade boys have a birthday in a summer month? _____

ii) How many total 7th grade girls have a birthday in a summer month? _____

iii) How many total 8th grade boys have a birthday in a summer month? _____

iv) How many total 8th grade girls have a birthday in a summer month? _____

v) Which two grades and genders have the same amount of students with birthdays in the summer months? _____

vi) What fraction of the summer month birthdays belong to 7th grade girls? _____

vii) What percent of the summer month birthdays belong to 8th grade girls? _____

viii) How many total boys birthdays are in the summer months? _____

ix) How many total girls birthdays are in the summer months? _____

x) In which month do an equal number of boys and girls in one grade share the same birthday? _____

xi) Which two months do the same amount of 8th grade girls have a birthday? _____

xii) What is the ratio of eighth grade girls' birthdays to seventh grade girls' birthdays? _____

xiii) What percent of total 7th grade girls' birthdays occur in June? _____

xiv) What percent of total 8th grade girls' birthdays occur in July? _____

xv) What is the ratio of 7th grade boys born in September to 8th grade boys born the same month? _____

xvi) What fraction of 8th grade boys have a birthday in June or July? _____

xvii) What is the ratio of 7th grade summer month birthdays to 8th grade summer month birthdays? _____

15a) **The following pie chart shows the result of a governor's election. It shows how many votes the candidate for each party received.**

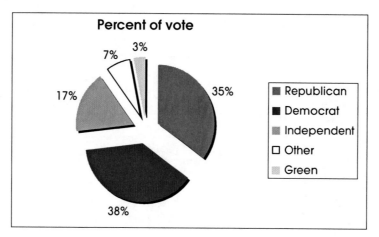

i) The largest amount of people voted for a candidate in which party? _____

ii) The smallest amount of people voted for a candidate in which party? _____

iii) About 55 percent of the people voted for which two parties? _____

iv) About 73 percent of the people voted for which two parties? _____

v) What percent of the people voted for either the Green Party candidate or an "other" candidate? _____

vi) Ten percent more voters voted for the Independent Party candidate than voted for the candidate from which party? _____

vii) What is the range of votes for this pie chart? _____

viii) What is the ratio of votes for Republican candidates to "other" candidates? _____

ix) How many more voters voted for the Republican candidate than the Independent candidate? _____

x) The difference in votes between what two groups is 21 percent? _____

xi) The number of votes received by the Green party candidate is equal to the difference in votes between what two parties? _____

xii) If 3000 people voted in this election, how many votes did the Green Party get? _____

xiii) If 3000 people voted in this election, how many votes did other parties get? _____

xiv) If 3000 people voted in this election, how many votes did the Independent Party get? _____

xv) If 3000 people voted in this election, how many votes did the Republican Party receive? _____

xvi) If 3000 people voted in this election, how many votes did the Democrat Party receive? _____

16a) Look at the train schedule from Millville to different destinations below.

Ex: A train arrives in Arrington 15 minutes before a train leaves for what city? **Boylston**

Leave	Time	Arrive	Estimated Time
Millville	11:00 AM	Arrington	12:45 PM
Millville	12:00 PM	Dover	2:00 PM
Millville	12:30 PM	Reading	2:45 PM
Millville	1:00 PM	Boylston	3:00 PM
Millville	1:45 PM	Bismarck City	3:30 PM
Millville	2:15 PM	Jefferson	3:50 PM

i) The train that leaves Millville to arrive in what city has the longest ride? _____

ii) The train that leaves Millville to arrive in what city has the shortest ride? _____

iii) How much longer after a train leaves Millville for Arrington does a train leave Millville for Dover? _____

iv) How many minutes is the ride between Millville and Reading? _____

v) The train for what city leaves 75 minutes before the train for Bismarck City? _____

vi) The train for what city arrives 65 minutes before a train arrives in Jefferson? _____

vii) The train ride between Millville and Dover takes how many minutes? _____

viii) A round trip ride between Millville and Arrington would probably take how long? _____

ix) Which trip takes 15 minutes less than the ride between Millville and Dover? _____

x) A train arrives in what city 15 minutes before the train leaves for Jefferson? _____

xi) A train leaves for Boylston 15 minutes after a train arrives in what city? _____

xii) A train leaves for Bismarck City 15 minutes before a train arrives in what city? _____

xiii) The trip between Millville and Boylston is 100 miles (160 km). How many minutes does it take the train, on average, to travel 50 miles (80 km)? _____

xiv) The trip between Millville and Dover is 120 miles (192 km). How many minutes does it take the train, on average, to travel 30 miles (48 km)? _____

xv) If the train to Jefferson City is 15 minutes late, what time will it arrive? _____

xvi) The train from Millville to Dover arrives with 10 percent of the estimated time left. What time did it arrive? _____

17a) Look at the following weather predications for the month of March below.

Ex: What is the median high temperature predicted for all five cities?

51°F (10.6°C)

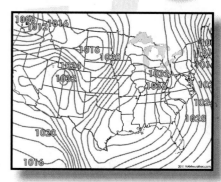

City	Predicted High	Predicted Low	Sky at day	Chance of precipitation
Chicago	34°F (1.1°C)	28°F (−2.2°C)	Mostly cloudy	25% chance of rain
Vancouver	51°F (10.6°C)	40°F (4.6°C)	Mostly sunny	5% chance of rain
Los Angeles	75°F (23.9°C)	58°F (14.4°C)	Mostly sunny	10% chance of rain
New York	36°F (2.2°C)	25°F (−3.9°C)	Cloudy	80% chance of snow
Orlando	82°F (27.8°C)	60°F (15.6°C)	Mostly cloudy	70% chance rain

i) Which city has the lowest predicted high temperature? _____

ii) Which city has the highest predicted low temperature? _____

iii) Which city is least likely to see precipitation? _____

iv) Which city is most likely to see precipitation? _____

v) Which city is most likely to see rain? _____

vi) What is the average predicted high for all five cities? _____

vii) What is the average predicted low for all five cities? _____

viii) What is the median temperature predicted for all five cities? _____

ix) What is the range in predicted high temperatures? _____

x) What is the range in predicted low temperatures? _____

xi) Which city is likely to see the most clouds? _____

xii) What is the ratio between Los Angeles predicted high and New York's predicted low in Fahrenheit? _____

xiii) The predicted high for Chicago is lower than the predicted low of which three cities? _____

xiv) Which city's predicted high is 3°F (19.5°C) more than twice the predicted high of New York? _____

xv) What is the mean predicted temperature for Orlando? _____

xvi) What is the mean predicted low of Chicago and Los Angeles? _____

NAME: _____

Review A

a) The line plot below shows how many students have each number of pets at home.

Mrs. Jones Class Pet Survey

	X							
	X	X						
	X	X	X					
X	X	X	X	X	X			
X	X	X	X	X	X	X		X
0 pets	1 pets	2 pets	3 pets	4 pets	5 pets	6 pets	7 pets	8 pets

i) How many students took this survey? _____

ii) How many students had no pets? _____

iii) How many more students had 1 pet than 8 pets? _____

iv) How many total students had more than 3 pets? _____

v) What is the mode of number of pets? _____

vi) What percent of the students have no pets? _____

vii) What percent of the students have 8 pets? _____

viii) What fraction of students own 2 pets? _____

ix) One-fourth of the students own how many pets? _____

x) The number of students who own four, five, or six pets is equal to the number of students who owns how many pets? _____

xi) Twice as many students own how many pets as own 4 pets? _____

xii) What is the ratio of students who own 3 pets to students who own 6 pets? _____

xiii) How many total pets does this class have? _____

xiv) What fraction of the total pets are owned by people who own 3 pets? _____

xv) What fraction of the total pets are owned by people who own 6 pets? _____

xvi) What is the average number of pets people had? _____

Data Analysis & Probability – Task & Drill Sheets CC3316

NAME: _____

Review B

a) **The graph below shows the number of students who play different instruments in the Carroll School band.**

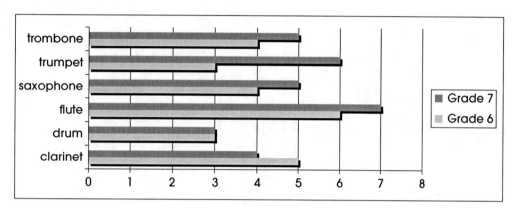

i) How many total sixth graders are in the band? _____

ii) How many total seventh graders are in the band? _____

iii) What instrument is played by the greatest number of sixth and seventh graders? _____

iv) What instrument is played by the least number of sixth and seventh graders? _____

v) What instrument is played by an equal number of sixth and seventh graders? _____

vi) How many more seventh graders play trombone than sixth graders? _____

vii) Which instrument is played by twice as many seventh graders as sixth graders? _____

viii) Which instrument is played by more sixth graders than seventh graders? _____

ix) What fraction of the sixth graders play clarinet? _____

x) What fraction of the seventh graders play saxophone? _____

xi) What is the ratio of sixth grade flute players to sixth grade drum players? _____

xii) What is the ratio of seventh grade clarinet players to seventh grade trumpet players? _____

xiii) What percent of the sixth graders play drums? _____

xiv) What percent of the seventh graders play trumpet? _____

xv) What percent of the total sixth and seventh graders play flute? _____

xvi) What percent of the total sixth and seventh graders play saxophone? _____

Review C

a) **The following column chart shows the number of boxes of each type of cookie sold for three different groups at the Wildlife Scout cookie sale.**

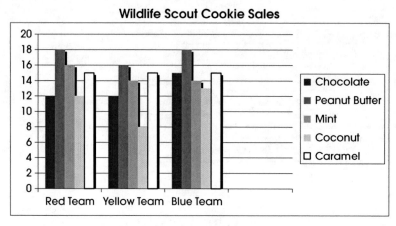

Wildlife Scout Cookie Sales

i) How many total cookie sales did the Red Team have? _____

ii) How many total cookie sales did the Yellow Team have? _____

iii) How many total cookie sales did the Blue Team have? _____

iv) Forty percent of the cookie sales for the Blue Team were
for which two cookies? _____

v) Thirty four cookie sales for the Red Team were which
two varieties? _____

vi) The Yellow Team had twice as many Peanut Butter cookie
sales as sales of which cookie? _____

vii) The Yellow Team and Red Team both had 12 of which cookie sales? _____

viii) The three teams had equal sales for which type of cookie? _____

ix) The Red Team had an equal number of which cookies sold? _____

x) The Blue Team has a 1:1 ratio in which two cookie sales? _____

xi) What is the ratio in Mint Cookie sales between the
Yellow Team and Blue Team? _____

xii) Twenty percent more of which cookies were sold by the
Red Team than Caramel cookies? _____

xiii) Which team had the smallest number of sales for
one type of cookie? _____

xiv) What is the ratio of Peanut Butter sales to Chocolate
sales for the red team? _____

xv) There is one less total sales of which cookies than there
were total sales of Caramel cookies for all three teams? _____

xvi) What is the average number of Chocolate cookie sales
for all three teams? _____

7.

1, 1, 4, 1, 2, 1, 2, 2, 3, 1

a) 13

b) 6

c) 12.67

d) 20

e) Answers may vary.

6.

Answers will vary.

4.

Answers will vary.

5.

Answers will vary.

3.

a) i) 3

ii) Answers may vary.

iii) 5

iv) Answers may vary.

b) Answers may vary.

c) Answers may vary.

2.

Answers will vary.

1.

a) i) $32.10

ii) There is no mode.

iii) Mean = $35.25,
Mode = $51.00

b) i) 6.25

ii) 6.2

iii) 4.17

c) i) 7

ii) 8

iii) 6

---

(9) (10) (11) (12) (13) (14) (15)

EZ✓

14.

Answers may vary.
Graph should reflect
the data collected.

12.

a) 1/5

b) 1/5

c) 1/5

d) 1/5

e) 1/5

f) 3/5

g) 2/5

h) Answers may vary.

(20)

13.

a) 3

b) 5

c) Answers may vary.

d) Answers may vary.

e) Answers may vary.

11.

Answers may vary.
Graph should reflect
the information given.

10.

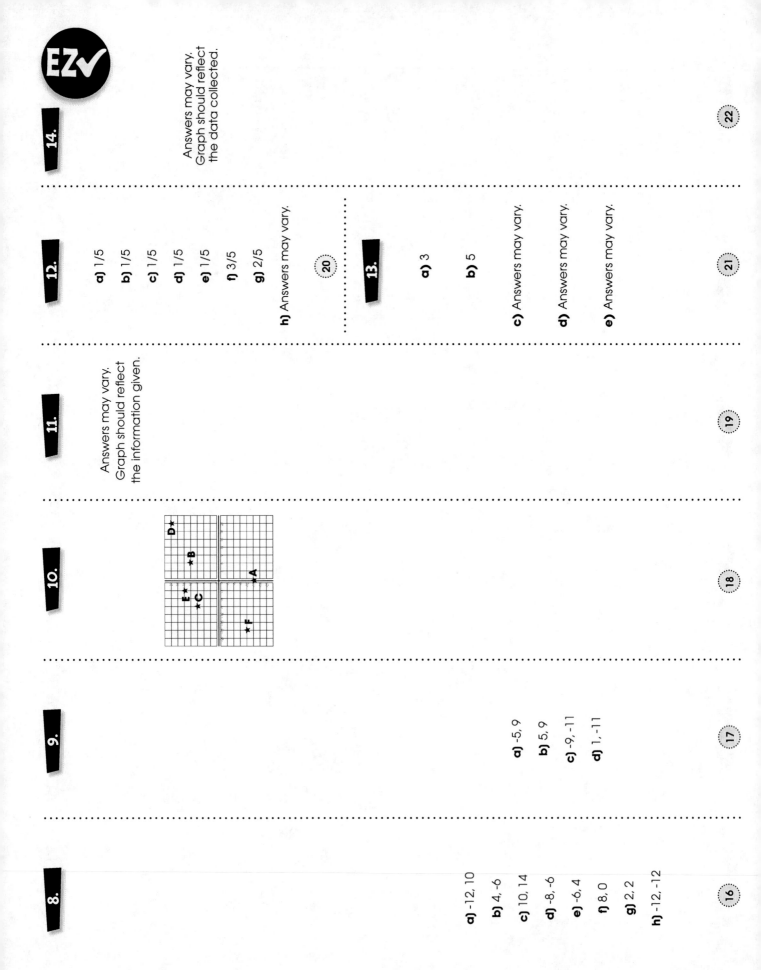

9.

a) -5, 9

b) 5, 9

c) -9, -11

d) 1, -11

8.

a) -12, 10

b) 4, -6

c) 10, 14

d) -8, -6

e) -6, 4

f) 8, 0

g) 2, 2

h) -12, -12

(22)

(21)

(19)

(18)

(17)

(16)

15.

a) 6.66

b) 8

c) 7

d) 10

e) Answers may vary.

f) Answers may vary.

g) Answers may vary.

h) Answers may vary.

Drill Sheet 1

a) v)

b) i)

c) iii)

d) iii)

e) iv)

f) v)

Drill Sheet 2

a) 1:56

b) 3:19

c) 10:27

d) 3:88

e) 12:23

f) Mean = 2:83,
Median = 2:77,
Mode = 1:56,
Range = 2:52

g) Answers may vary.

h) Answers may vary.

Review A

a) 12/20, 60%

b) 6/20, 30%

c) 2/20, 10%

d) 8/20, 40%

e) Answers may vary.

Review B

Answers will vary.

Review C

a) Answers may vary.

b) Most = chocolate;
Least = granola bars
and yogurt

c) Answers may vary.

d) 21%

EZ✓

23   24   25   26   27   28

EZ✓

6.

Answers will vary.

6A

5.

a) Playing Games

b) Eating Snacks

c) Answers may vary. Possible answer includes: values.

d) Answers may vary. Possible answers include: values, headings, and time.

5A

4.

Answers will vary.

4A

3.

a) i) Mean = 12, Mode = none

ii) Median = 12, Range = 18

b) i) Mean = 6, Mode = 2

ii) Median = 4, Range = 14

iii) Outlier = 16

iv) Answers may vary.

c) Answers may vary.

d) i) Danya = none, Lorna = none

ii) Danya = 1.47, Lorna = 1.31

iii) Danya = 1.36, Lorna = 1.25

3A

2.

Answers will vary.

2A

1.

a) 31°C (87°F)

b) 32°C (90°F)

c) 32°C (90°F)

d) 7 (12)

e) No

f) 56%, Likely

g) Answers may vary.

h) Answers may vary.

1A

1.

a)
i) 19
ii) 20
iii) 20
iv) 3
v) 6
vi) 17
vii) Ms. Li's and Mr. Crocker's class
viii) 2 more
ix) Pumpkin
x) 2 more students
xi) 2 more students
xii) 10
xiii) Mrs. Smythe and Ms. Li
xiv) Apple
xv) Cream
xvi) 8 students

29

2.

a)
i) Arthur
ii) Carla
iii) 1.83 minutes
iv) 5.5 min/mile (3.44 min/km)
v) 5.63 min/mile (3.52 min/km)
vi) 0.34 min
vii) 27.45 min
viii) 28.15 min
ix) 0.7 min
x) 27.54 min
xi) Jessica and Leigh
xii) Ariel
xiii) 0.2 min
xiv) Miguel
xv) Tim
xvi) Chelsea

30

3.

a)
i) baseball
ii) glove
iii) 7 items
iv) baseballs
v) 10%
vi) 20%
vii) 30%
viii) 40%
ix) 4:3
x) 3:2
xi) helmets
xii) 2/10
xiii) baseball and bats
xiv) 1/3
xv) baseballs, helmets and bats
xvi) baseballs, helmets and bats

31

4.

a)
i) Alice Jenkins
ii) Tom Quincy
iii) Caleb Wallace and Samuel Owens
iv) Alice Jenkins
v) Caleb Wallace and Samuel Owens
vi) Tom Quincy
vii) 2/5
viii) 1/4
ix) 1/4
x) 1/10
xi) 900 votes
xii) 1440 votes
xiii) 900 votes
xiv) 360
xv) 5%
xvi) 80%

32

5.

a)
i) Los Angeles
ii) Chicago
iii) Dallas
iv) Vancouver
v) 0.3°F (0.2°C)
vi) 35.1°F (19.5°C)
vii) 70.6°F (21.4°C)
viii) 59.5°F (15.3°C)
ix) Dallas
x) 54.4°F (12.5°C)
xi) New York City
xii) Boston
xiii) Boston
xiv) 36.54 in (928.13 mm)
xv) Vancouver
xvi) Chicago

33

6.

a)
i) 3 students
ii) 2 more students
iii) 1 student
iv) Question 9
v) Question 2
vi) 3 students
vii) 3 students
viii) 26 students
ix) 26 students
x) 1:1
xi) 5 students
xii) Question 4 and 8
xiii) Question 6
xiv) Question 9
xv) Question 1 and 3
xvi) 20 students

34

7.

a)
i) Chocolate
ii) Chocolate
iii) Other
iv) Strawberry
v) 21 students
vi) 21 students
vii) 1/7
viii) 1/3
ix) Vanilla
x) 7:6
xi) 4 students
xii) Chocolate
xiii) Vanilla and Mint
xiv) Vanilla
xv) 5 students
xvi) Mint

35

EZ✓

8.

a)
i) 8 players
ii) Gabe Carter
iii) 28 minutes
iv) 23.75 minutes
v) Dave Drew
vi) 75 points
vii) Greg Kidd and Gabe Carter
viii) Paul Allen, Greg Kidd and Gabe Carter
ix) 15:10
x) Greg Kidd
xi) 40 rebounds
xii) 5 rebounds
xiii) Jake Smith
xiv) 8 assists
xv) Paul Allen
xvi) 2.5 assists

36

9.

a)
i) Saturday
ii) Friday
iii) 40°F (4.5°C)
iv) 39°F (4°C)
v) 8:00 pm
vi) 11:00 pm
vii) 12°F (7°C)
viii) 11°F (6°C)
ix) 11.5°F (6.5°C)
x) Friday
xi) 2°F (1°C)
xii) 8:00 pm and 9:00 pm
xiii) 7:00 pm and 8:00 pm
xiv) Friday
xv) 7°F (4°C)
xvi) drops 2°F (1°C) each hour

37

10.

a)
i) Jessica
ii) Carmen
iii) 55 votes
iv) Carmen
v) Michael
vi) Antoine
vii) Carmen and Won
viii) 11 votes
ix) Jessica and Antoine
x) Michael
xi) Carmen and Won
xii) Won
xiii) 8 votes
xiv) Jessica
xv) 44 votes
xvi) 9:15

38

11.

a)
i) Hockey Stick and Basketball Sneakers
ii) Baseballs
iii) Hockey Gloves
iv) Baseballs
v) Basketball Hoop
vi) Hockey Gloves and Basketball Hoop
vii) Basketball Sneakers
viii) Basketball Hoop
ix) Baseball Bats and Football
x) Baseball Helmets and Baseballs
xi) Basketballs and Baseball Bats
xii) Baseballs cost 1/10 Hockey Stick and Basketball Sneakers
xiii) Basketball Hoop
xiv) 50:40
xv) $22.00 mode
xvi) $61.00 range

39

12.

a)
i) 1 in 2
ii) 1 in 2
iii) 1:1
iv) 40%
v) 30%
vi) 30%
vii) 70%
viii) 30%
ix) 3:7
x) 40%
xi) 3 in 10
xii) 2 in 10 or 1 in 5
xiii) 2 in 10 or 1 in 5
xiv) 1 in 10
xv) white square with odd number
xvi) square with white letters

40

13.

a)
i) 97 desserts
ii) 65 pieces of fruit
iii) 45 bagels
iv) Monday and Thursday
v) Friday
vi) Tuesday
vii) Monday
viii) Tuesday and Wednesday
ix) Friday
x) Dessert
xi) Bagel
xii) 15 mode
xiii) Thursday
xiv) 19.4 desserts
xv) Wednesday
xvi) Tuesday and Wednesday

41

14.

a)
i) 22 boys
ii) 20 girls
iii) 22 boys
iv) 18 girls
v) Grade 7 and 8 boys
vi) 10/41
vii) 22%
viii) 44 boys
ix) 38 girls
x) August
xi) June and July
xii) 9:10
xiii) 25%
xiv) 22%
xv) 1:1
xvi) 1/2
xvii) 21:20

42

15.

a)
i) Democrat
ii) Green
iii) Democrat and Independent
iv) Republican and Democrat
v) 10%
vi) Other
vii) 35% votes
viii) 5:1
ix) 18% voters
x) Independent and Democrat
xi) Republican and Democrat
xii) 90 votes
xiii) 210 votes
xiv) 510 votes
xv) 1050 votes
xvi) 1140 votes

16.

a)
i) Reading
ii) Jefferson
iii) 1 hour
iv) 135 min
v) Reading
vi) Reading
vii) 120 min
viii) 3 hours and 30 min or 210 min
ix) Arrington and Bismarck City
x) Dover
xi) Arrington
xii) Dover
xiii) 60 min
xiv) 30 min
xv) 4:15 pm
xvi) 1:48 pm

44

17.

a)
i) Chicago
ii) Orlando
iii) Vancouver
iv) New York
v) Orlando
vi) 55.6°F (13.12°C)
vii) 42.2°F (28.5°C)
viii) 45.5°F (7.6°C) median
ix) 48°F (26.7°C) range
x) 35°F (19.5°C) range
xi) New York
xii) 3:1
xiii) Vancouver, Los Angeles and Orlando
xiv) Los Angeles
xv) 71°F (21.7°C)
xvi) 43°F (6.1°C)

45

Review A

a)
i) 20 students
ii) 2 students
iii) 4 students
iv) 6 students
v) 0, 4 and 5 pets
vi) 10%
vii) 5%
viii) 1/5
ix) 1 pet
x) 1 pet
xi) 2 pets
xii) 3:1
xiii) 54 pets
xiv) 1/6
xv) 1/9
xvi) 2.7 pets

46

Review B

a)
i) 25 students
ii) 30 students
iii) Flute
iv) Drum
v) Drum
vi) 1 more
vii) Trumpet
viii) Clarinet
ix) 1/5
x) 1/6
xi) 2:1
xii) 2:3
xiii) 12%
xiv) 20%
xv) 23.6%
xvi) 16.4%

47

Review C

a)
i) 61 sales
ii) 51 sales
iii) 75 sales
iv) Chocolate and Caramel
v) Peanut Butter and Mint
vi) Coconut
vii) Chocolate
viii) Caramel
ix) Chocolate and Coconut
x) Chocolate and Caramel
xi) 1:1
xii) Peanut Butter
xiii) Yellow Team
xiv) 3:2
xv) Mint
xvi) 13 sales

48

© CLASSROOM COMPLETE PRESS

Data Analysis & Probability – Task & Drill Sheets CC3316

(these answers are for the 6 free bonus pages, see page 5 for download instructions)

6.
a)
i) 158
ii) 53 students
iii) 6 more students
iv) Salad
v) Subs in grade 6
vi) Hamburger in grade 8
vii) Sub
viii) Pizza and Sub
ix) 7:4
x) Salad in grade 6 and 8
xi) 8:7
xii) 2/7
xiii) 11 students
xiv) 14 students
xv) 20 students
xvi) 7 students

6A

5.
a)
i) 7/12
ii) 5/12
iii) 1/4
iv) 1/6
v) 5 in 12
vi) 4 in 12 or 1 in 3
vii) 6 in 12 or 1 in 2
viii) Circle
ix) Hexagon
x) 8.3% chance
xi) 16.7% chance
xii) 33.3% chance
xiii) 1:1
xiv) 2:1
xv) 7:5
xvi) 2:1

5A

4.
a)
i) 80 respondents
ii) 45% male
iii) 55% female
iv) Other
v) 3:2
vi) 3 more students
vii) Science and History
viii) 3/8
ix) 58 students
x) 1/8
xi) 60%
xii) 70 students
xiii) 27.5%
xiv) 5:24
xv) 68.75%
xvi) 31.25%

4A

3.
a)
Answers will vary. More snow fell in December 2009 than December 2010. Students might notice the same amount of snow fell on December 8. Two more inches of snow fell on December 9, 2010, than December 9, 2009.

3A

2.
a)
i) Chen
ii) Thomas
iii) Chen
iv) Erin
v) Thomas
vi) 70
vii) 120
viii) 58.3%
ix) Jessica and Gabe
x) 5:4
xi) 3/5
xii) Chen
xiii) Thomas
xiv) Erin
xv) Chen
xvi) 41.7%

2A

1.
a)
i) 1 in 8
ii) 2 in 8 or 1 in 4
iii) 2 in 8 or 1 in 4
iv) 3 in 8
v) 2 in 8 or 1 in 4
vi) 1 in 8
vii) 2 in 8 or 1 in 4
viii) 5 in 8
ix) 3 in 8
x) 5:3
xi) 2:1
xii) odd numbers
xiii) consonants
xiv) 1/4
xv) 1/4
xvi) 1/2

1A